A **Maker's** Guide to

LEVERS

Written by JOHN WOOD

Illustrated by AMY LI

LERNER PUBLICATIONS ◆ MINNEAPOLIS

First American edition published in 2021 by Lerner Publishing Group, Inc.

Editor: Madeline Tyler
Design: Drue Rintoul

Lerner Publications Company
An imprint of Lerner Publishing Group, Inc.
241 First Avenue North
Minneapolis, MN 55401 USA

For reading levels and more information, look up this title at www.lernerbooks.com.

Main body text set in VAG Rounded Std. Typeface provided by Adobe Systems.

Library of Congress Cataloging-in-Publication Data

Names: Wood, John, 1990– author. | Li, Amy, illustrator.
Title: A maker's guide to levers / written by John Wood ; illustrated by Amy Li.
Other titles: Levers
Description: First American edition. | Minneapolis : Lerner Publications, 2021. | Series: A maker's guide to simple machines |
  Includes index. | Audience: Ages 6–10 | Audience: Grades 2–3 | Summary: "A smart but silly alien companion and
  toy-making activity make learning about levers tons of fun! Readers can discover how levers work and the types of levers
  we see in our everyday lives"—Provided by publisher.
Identifiers: LCCN 2020054236 (print) | LCCN 2020054237 (ebook) | ISBN 9781728416427 (lib. bdg.) | ISBN 9781728438313 (pbk.) |
  ISBN 9781728418872 (eb pdf)
Subjects: LCSH: Levers—Juvenile literature.
Classification: LCC TJ207 .W66 2021 (print) | LCC TJ207 (ebook) | DDC 621.8—dc23

LC record available at https://lccn.loc.gov/2020054236
LC ebook record available at https://lccn.loc.gov/2020054237

Manufactured in the United States of America
1-48889-49203-12/21/2020

Table of CONTENTS

Words that look like <u>this</u> can be found in the glossary on page 24.

BE A MAKER

Oh dear. This is Maker. It looks like he has made a huge mess. We are so sorry.

Believe it or not, Maker is very smart when it comes to machines.

A machine is an object that makes a job easier to do. Maker wants to teach you about one of the simplest types of machine: a lever.

A yo-yo is a type of simple machine.

LEVERS

Levers are long and hard. They can be anything from a wooden plank to a metal handle. Levers move around a fixed point.

A seesaw is a very simple lever. The long thin part is called a beam. This beam is made of metal.

Some simple machines are made of more than one lever. For example, scissors are made up of two levers working together. They both move around the same <u>fixed</u> point.

FIXED POINT

Levers are usually made of something that doesn't bend, such as metal, wood, or hard plastic.

Levers are all around us. Let's look at some more.

The handles you use to brake on a bike are levers.

Stapler

Boat oars

Hockey stick

PARTS OF A LEVER

There is more to a lever than just a long piece of metal or wood! There is also a load. This is the thing you want to move. The pivot is the fixed point that the lever moves around.

Beam

Load

Pivot

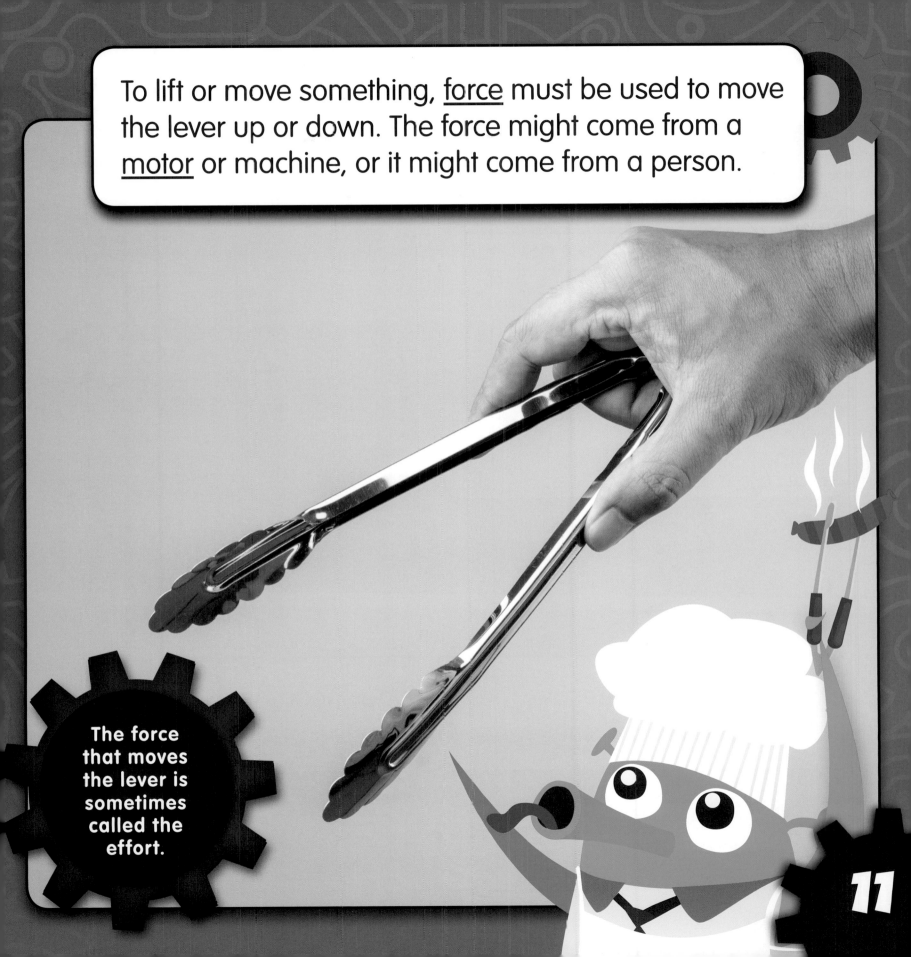

To lift or move something, <u>force</u> must be used to move the lever up or down. The force might come from a <u>motor</u> or machine, or it might come from a person.

The force that moves the lever is sometimes called the effort.

11

HOW A LEVER WORKS

The longer the lever is, the less force is needed to lift something. Look at this seesaw. On one side is a heavy load. Maker is on the other side. He is light.

Load

To <u>balance</u> the seesaw, the load goes near the pivot, and Maker goes far away from the pivot.

CLASSES OF LEVER

There are three <u>classes</u> of lever. But what makes them different?

HLAFFLEPLAFFPLAFF.

Maker says it is all about the order of the load, pivot, and effort.

Remember, the load is the thing you want to lift, the pivot is the fixed point, and the effort is whatever is doing all the work—for example, a person!

The order of a class one lever is effort, pivot, load. Remember, the important thing is that the pivot is in the middle.

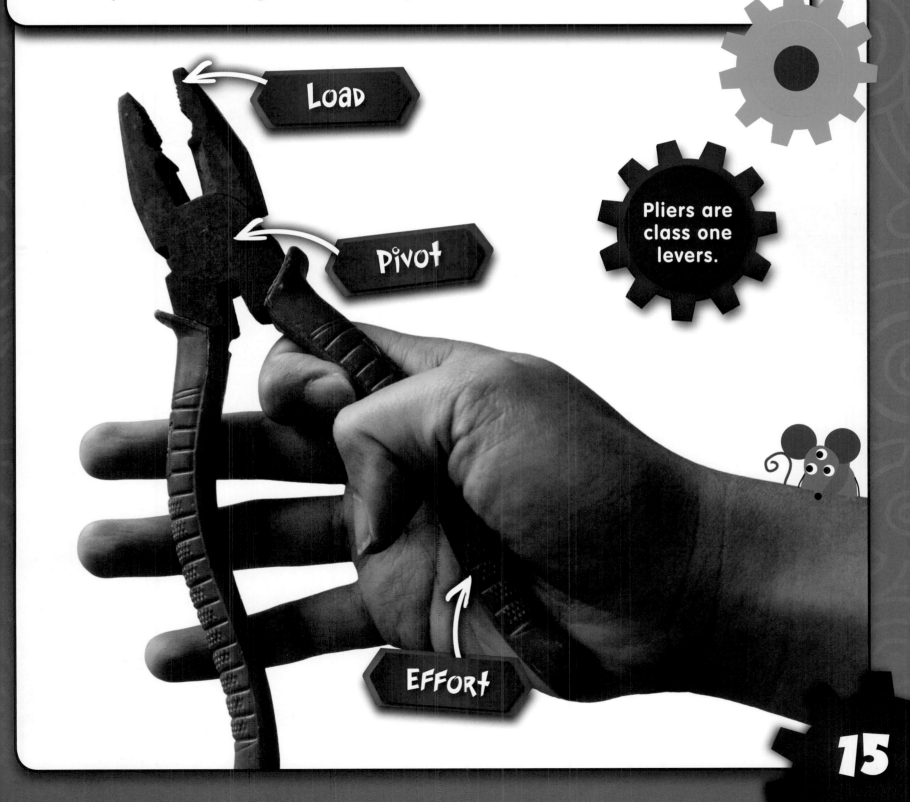

Load

Pivot

Pliers are class one levers.

EFFORT

15

The order of a class two lever is effort, load, pivot.
The closer the load is to the pivot, the easier it is to lift.

EFFORT

LOAD

Pivot

Wheelbarrows are class two levers.

The order of a class three lever is pivot, effort, load. When someone holds the handle of this lever, it acts like a pivot. The hand in the middle makes the lever move.

Shovels are class three levers.

LOAD

PIVOT

EFFORT

BUILD A CATAPULT

It is time to build! We will be using levers to make a toy catapult. We will try and fire something into a paper cup.

The catapult will use a class one lever.

- 8 small craft sticks
- 2 larger craft sticks
- 3 rubber bands
- Glue

- 1 plastic bottlecap
- Paper cup
- Some small, soft things to fire, such as pom-pom balls

Stack your eight small sticks on top of each other.

Put rubber bands around each end of the stack. You might need to loop the rubber bands around a few times so they are nice and tight.

Slide the end of a big stick between the bottom two sticks in the stack.

STEP 4

Line up the other big stick as shown in the picture. One end of this stick should be touching one end of the first big stick.

21

Put a rubber band around the ends of the two big sticks. Slide the stack toward that rubber band.

STEP 6

Glue the bottlecap to the end of the top large craft stick.

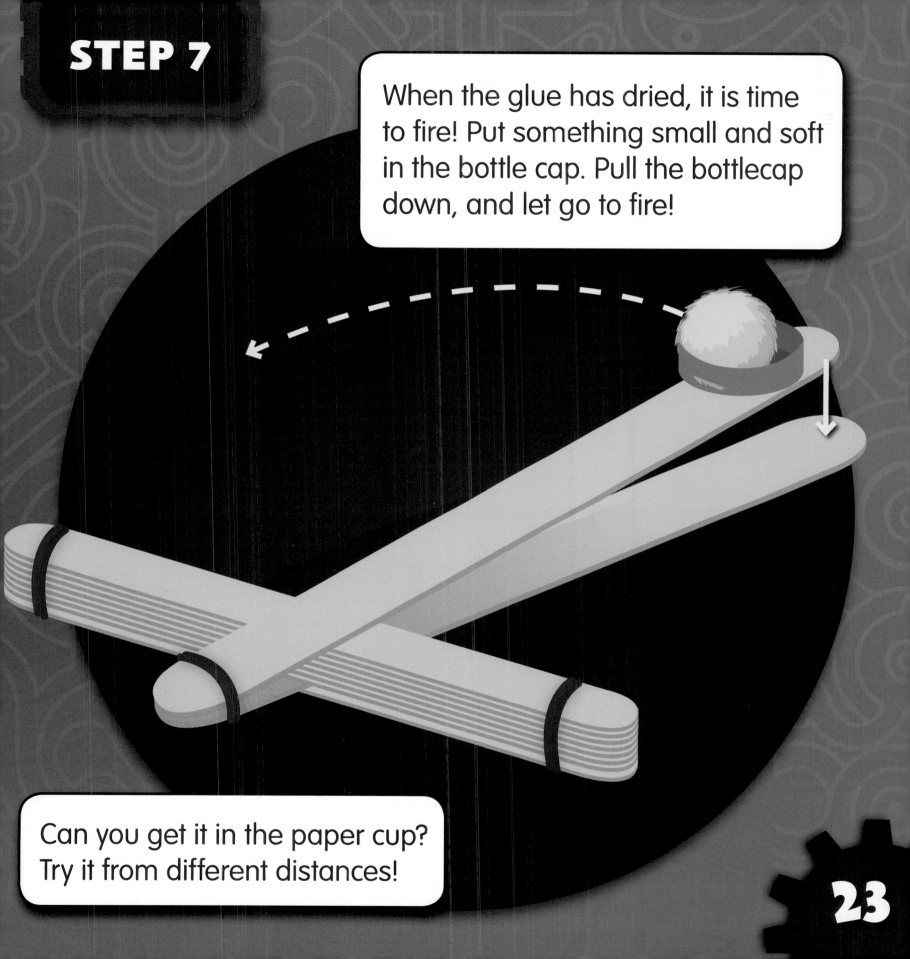

When the glue has dried, it is time to fire! Put something small and soft in the bottle cap. Pull the bottlecap down, and let go to fire!

Can you get it in the paper cup? Try it from different distances!

GLOSSARY

balance	even on both sides
classes	types
fixed	not moving
force	a push or pull on an object
motor	a machine that moves things

INDEX

24